here, there, nowhere

Adina Vlasov

Presentation by *BookLeaf Publishing*

Web: www.bookleafpub.com

E-mail: info@bookleafpub.com

ISBN: 9789357445399

First edition 2021

DEDICATION

To CJ, my long-time believer in my art.

on poetry

it's pouring out of me
and i can't stop it

how have i been away from this space for so
long?
it claws at every last heartstring

the flood of feelings begging
"release me",

    "release me",

        "release me"

greatness is not a requirement
    to Do.

strip

into the trenches:
soul sky, royal blue
infinite wells of emotion

each creation channelled
wrapped neatly with a bow
pretty packages i hold dear

with you i share these starry slivers
an act so intimate
it belongs in the bedroom

shell (2.0)

on my best days i am but a shell

if you ask who i am
there will be no answer
but hold me to your ear
and you'll hear whispers of yesterday:

the loves and laurels
structures holding me up:
a confidence within confines

but in the open ocean?

i am at the mercy of the tides
    (the moon, my mood)
i used to think i was so special
feeling so much, so deeply
convinced no one else understood

but of course they do
we all feel
i just do nothing but.

friendly fire

a welcoming cry for love from afar
with nonchalant neglect of nearness.
mistaking kindness for care
and tension for war;
a dangerous defect in process

believing in immutability,
i trust without trying
lines blur and years blur
and solid ground is a myth.

until those who were mine float out
and those who are not swim in
until there is only the Middle:
too far to connect; to close to forget

questions & musings

awake beyond my limits
going inwards,
          wallowing,
3a.m. sitting in the solitude
but the one desire is to connect
with someone
who will care, love, nurture, notice, embrace,
protect -
have a deep love for every last part of
my being

is it my ego?
do i think i am so special
to be so cherished -
would anyone really do that?

would i really do that for someone?

//

am i not getting something vital?
a type of attention that is moreso being seen

for myself.

do i think he doesn't see me for who i am?

possibly (probably).

is it because he doesn't tell me what he sees?

does such a person exits, who tells you these
things?
am i supposed to be that person for myself?

probably (possibly).

could i ever leave?
i'm afraid the answer is pretty much no.
i don't know

that seems to be the resounding chorus of my
recent life:
"i don't know"

gardener

i am always watering the wrong garden

leaving the buds who will gladly blossom for me
untended
and yet they try,
reaching their tender tendrils up t'wards me; up
t'wards God
and whilst He says
"grow my loves, you are meant for each other"

i am watering the wrong garden

infertile soil, grounds for death
i gladly pour my heart into
and weep when years' worth of pouring and
pouring
yield no harvest

i take it personally.

but miracles and pitfalls of nature are not my
jurisdiction
daisies grow where roses die
God knows what I do not

i am watering the wrong garden

memoir of love in a golden hour

the sadness comes right on schedule this year:
it is November and i weep for the memories
we'll never make

we are driving on familiar streets when you tell
me it's over
suddenly the sun is too bright and the music too
loud

i feel empty and grey so i call out of work and
run to you crying
you buy me soup and that night we make love.

i can't recall the last time i ate breakfast alone.
i know your kitchen cupboards better than mine.

early afternoons we step out into the real world.
in the crisp fall sunlight we are born anew.

foolish

how scary to think
that with a single glance
or touch
or word
you make me burst with happiness
or shatter from grief

how scary to think
that i would drop my world
to be with you
yet you, so nonchalant
hold yours tight; shared
but not given

how foolish am i
to give you the power
to love me
to hurt me
to hold and remold me
into an extension of you

how foolish am i
to think i stand a chance
with a man
when i am just a girl;
a stumbling child
afraid of the dark

deja vu

in that moment i knew it was over

let's play a blame game:
pin the tail on
me

what was i even looking for in you?

(haiku)

how to be social:
ingest alcohol; smile, wave
who are these people?

August

August brings with it a dormant chill
       familiar but forgotten
i once again doubt i can handle things i have
handled
       many times before.

just for a moment July held me -
       a cocoon of comfort
dog days stretching out,
       life in blissful amber

days grow shorter and in the distance -
       life: looming.
she gets closer every day

       can i ever outrun her?

here, there, nowhere

detached and growing
further away from concrete
roots shrivel;
reality fizzles
it's a hazy afternoon

the past is flowing
i haven't felt ground in weeks
loose petals;
or screws, metals
stuck inside a cartoon

intact and glowing
the trick of the light is brief
vines linking;
smiles syncing
i promise i'll come home soon.

premature

a release from carnage
needs not met
even before time started ticking

not complete
rug ripped out from under
turning circles begging for bread

the magic
          (or science,
          just magic by another name)
by which we become:

built from blocks
insides growing inside
safe houses (some)
erratic homes (others)

rest

a scream into the void
a note in Life's symphony
our house of hay imploding
but who is the wolf at the door?

neither fear nor fire is the question or answer
both are too extreme
peace is the default state of Earth
nature's Grand Conductor knows only
equilibrium

it is only us - when we have so lost our way
who bring turmoil and war into the world
and into ourselves

it is only us - when we think ourselves unique
and important
who create divides and barriers for our kin
where once were wide open spaces

we fight and fidget
          for what?
let us rest,
holding hands with our siblings
as the music plays on.

a fly at a wedding

a poem cannot in good faith encompass
		my feelings of joy and mourning that
ebb and flow
as you entwine eternally with the man of your
dreams
		whilst i sit on my floor among lists and
laundry

i am a fly on the wall,
		through a screen
on a day i had always dreamed i'd spend beside
you

because i love you unflinchingly even as years
have passed
		and lives have drifted
even as we haven't spoken in months.

but of course, it must have been my fault
it seems a recurring pattern that i drift to the
edges and eventually off the cliffs
		of my dearest friends' minds and hearts.

but it's not about me.

and as the rings slip on and the words ring out:
"I do."
joy washes over me
and i pray for you
          smile for you, cry for you
I do.

because it's about you.
beautiful, magical, graceful, ever-loving you.

to me, you are still my best friend.
and if that isn't true for you, that's okay.
i will hurt,
          alone.
and it will be right.

because you are love, and love is you.

and it's about you.

17

to be a good woman

the ease of shrinking
intimate inanimacy
put on a pretty pedestal
for a pageant crowd of one

a personal preference
to see through someone else's eyes
this curated caricature
2-D darling;
effortless effigy

the ease of thinking
foreign fancies
adopting dreams, schemes, and plans
not my own, but of a man's

"sure, I'll hold"

a beaten path

i swear in this one

how many bottles of wine do i have to consume
to feel i've accomplished something?

what is being an artist?

this label, so irreverent
frankly irrelevant
dependent
on the balancing act of
intangible, fickle creativity
and finalized concrete creation

i am not content
making "content"
what the fuck is "content"?
      (what the fuck is being content?)

implied consumption.
all of us baby birds
opening wide
eagerly anticipating
regurgitated, never-ending streams
of bastardized art-vomit

fuck.

purgatory

is this purgatory?
why am i holding us hostage?
for fear of flying?
the truth is not a tether

all this back and forth
negotiating nothings
         until everything flattens out
a waveless sea

white walls; white noise

how do we proceed in this abyss?
when we don't know left from right?
up from down?
together from apart?

hold my hand as we fall

to sleep alone again

the first day i stretch out:
taking up the space i hadn't filled in years
starfish on a sandbank
blanket of warm waves

the second day i venture to the other side:
closer to the things i need -
the things i've been reaching for
the sun is shining and the barrier's broken

the third day i curl up
returning to my origins
a fraction of feelings
i do not need the whole sea

mirror

spilled milk
sweet and nourishing
the ruse is up;
we lap at it like kittens

your moonlight mouth
the way i don't expect to fit -
the surprise when i do
time spent on my toes

the newness of our
brittle boundaries
already at the crux of comfort
won't you lay with me awhile?

alone together
not lost, just looking
i am a mirror
but not this time

conversations with myself

falling back in love with myself. dusting her off and asking "how are you?" it's been a deep sleep. reacquainted with the joy of being. sunbeams on a tree-lined street. to think i could have been existing in warmth this whole time. iced coffee on fall mornings. treating myself the way i'd like to be treated. letting creativity cushion the blow of letting go. it's pouring out of me and i can't stop it. doors are opening and closing, over and over. there is so much space for love to enter.

you can say i love you a thousand times and never have a drop of it.
now, a flood.

"i'm well. it's good to be back."